ENDORSEMENTS

"I can't even begin to explain how excellent this curriculum is for my homeschooling children. It is perfect for a wide age range. It is beautifully illustrated. It sparks curiosity as it inspires my children to look deeply into God's Word. This curriculum builds up their faith and gives them a biblical perspective of science and teaches them to think outside the box."

— **Sarah Janisse Brown**
Founder of The Thinking Tree; Creator of Dyslexia Games; Homeschooling Mom

"Your kids will not want to miss out on this adventure! Dino Dave masterfully leads us on a journey pointing out God's handiwork from the smallest of organisms to the greatest of natural wonders. On every page, he demonstrates that the Bible is wonderful and infallible. This book would be a blessing for your family worship time. However, I'm not sure who will love this book more: the kids or the parents."

— **Ben Lamphere**
Pastor for Family Ministries at Trinity Baptist Church, Concord, NH

"Dino Dave's Adventures in Apologetics is fresh and up-to-date. It presents some of the best modern apologetics in a captivating way that I think will help make these creationist arguments more accessible to children."

— **Dr. John Morris**
President Emeritus of the Institute for Creation Research

"David Woetzel (Dino Dave) has done an amazing job explaining the scientific discoveries and examining the fossil record and then communicating this in such a way for a child to understand. This book can be enjoyed by children and parents alike while providing the tools to give a defense for the reason for the hope that a child has in their belief in a loving Creator God and in their Savior Jesus Christ. These stories will captivate the mind and imagination with TRUTH. I highly recommend this book to be a part of every Christian family's library."

— **Mark Lester**
Board Chair, Child Evangelism Fellowship of NH

"The elementary age children at our church were fascinated by these apologetic lessons! Dino Dave does a wonderful job of choosing captivating topics and providing answers to difficult questions. Repeatedly, your child will be directed back to the one source of truth, the Bible, through these lessons. A Biblical worldview is an imperative foundation for a child, and the ability to decipher truth is essential to a Christ follower. These lessons will put our Creator's amazing design on display, capture the intrigue of a child, provide truth and strengthen faith!"

— **Cheryl Bagwell**
Director of Children's Ministries, Calvary Baptist Church, Simpsonville, SC

"Dino Dave gives children an engaging story of his travels around the world to learn about dinosaurs, fossils, and Noah's Flood. Reading his adventures will help children understand evidence that the Bible is true. Children will also enjoy learning about dinosaurs, as well as other huge creatures that once lived. Most importantly, his adventures will teach children more about God and His creation."

— **Dr. Kevin Anderson**
Director of Creation Research Society

DINO DAVE's ADVENTURES

in apologetics

BOOK 2

by Dave Woetzel

First Printing: April 2022

ISBN: 978-0-578-81041-6

Library of Congress Control Number: 2020925873

Please consider requesting that a copy of this volume be purchased by your local library system.
All Scripture is from the King James Version of the Bible.

Printed in China

For information contact:

www.GenesisPark.com

ACKNOWLEDGMENTS & DEDICATION

Special thanks to Kaylee Kelso for extensive design and layout work and to Lorraine McKeever for proofreading.

This book is dedicated to all those in my family who have invested in little lives by being schoolteachers: Patty, Todd, Becky, Laura, Charity, & Heidi.

DINO DAVE'S ADVENTURES
table of contents

AUTHOR'S INTRODUCTION

This book came out of a sincere desire to drive home to elementary students the reality of the stories in the Bible. For decades my wife, Gloria, and I have traveled around the United States and other countries speaking on apologetics topics: creation, the Genesis Flood and God's amazing dinosaurians. Gloria's primary ministry has been with the youngest students (Kindergarten to 5th grade). She found that a number of these children enjoy the Bible stories they learn in Sunday School. But they consider them merely wonderful stories, like the clever fictional stories they read about in children's books. This contrasts with the things that they learn in school, instructional narratives that are real, historically and scientifically accurate. Too many of these children will grow up to become skeptical of the Bible, abandoning their childhood faith and embracing the materialistic secular culture around them.

Dino Dave's Adventures in Apologetics is a compilation of stories based on real events in my life. You will find the stories full of real people, real places, real field research, real historical narratives, real photos (mostly) and real scientific facts. Hopefully this book can make a difference by equipping young children with fun-filled, simply-presented arguments that buttress the Christian faith and authority of God's Word. Each adventure starts with a parenthetical statement of the focus of the story. It is meant to inform the teacher of the key point I am aiming at, so they can elaborate further, if they wish, and drive that lesson home. Brightly-colored Bible verses are sprinkled throughout the stories because the words of scripture themselves have a power to profoundly touch our lives.

I hope that you enjoy these simple stories and can passionately share them with the precious children in your life!

—Dino Dave

DINO DAVE & THE CRYPTID CHAMP

(Lesson: Plesiosaurs lived alongside man and some "hidden animals" may still be alive today!)

The title of this story has a strange word in it. What is a cryptid? The word "cryptid" means hidden animal. They are animals that are not yet proven by science to exist. Sometimes when people tell stories about new animals that they think they saw; it turns out to be just a mistake. But other times some amazing animals are discovered by explorers. These animals existed all along. Because we didn't know about them, they are new to us. They were cryptids (hidden animals) until someone found them and showed them to scientists. This story is about a special cryptid named Champ.

One Sunday, while Dino Dave was at church, the pastor spoke on the wisdom of God. God is so much smarter than we are. He knows everything and we can't hide from Him. The Bible says that there is no creature that is hidden from His sight (Hebrews 4:13). Sometimes God wisely decides to hide things from us, and we do not always understand what He is doing. Other times He chooses to show us new things.

Hiding in bed

"The secret things belong unto the LORD our God: but those things which are revealed belong unto us and to our children for ever," (Deuteronomy 29:29).

After church, Dino Dave met Garth, a man with a friendly smile, a bald head, and a big mustache. They talked together and found out that they both like dinosaurs. But Garth did not think that a big creature, like a dinosaur,

Dino Dave and Garth

Philippine monitor lizard

could still be alive – hidden after all these years of scientific exploration. "Wouldn't a big animal like a dinosaur have been found already with so many people living on the Earth?" asked Garth. Dino Dave told Garth that new kinds of animals are still being found every year. In the year 2009, a new type of large lizard was discovered in the country of the Philippines. This monitor lizard had been seen by tribal hunters. Even though it lives up in the trees and eats mostly fruit and snails, it grows to almost 7 feet long! How did scientists find this hidden animal? Well, they talked to people who lived there and learned where to search for the huge lizard. But it still took months of research work before they were able to catch a living monitor lizard.

Garth listened carefully and was getting interested in cryptids. He wanted to know where cryptid animals might still be hiding. Dino Dave told him that the deep ocean is the biggest unexplored area on Earth. Some interesting kinds of sea monsters might still be there, waiting to be found. "Would the sea monster look like a dinosaur?" wondered Garth. Dino Dave told him about the bones of a swimming monster that have been found. From the fossils, we know it looked like a long-necked dinosaur, but it had flippers in the place of legs. It is called a plesiosaur. Garth was excited, "Do you really believe plesiosaurs might still be alive today in the ocean or deep lakes?"

Dino Dave explained that evolutionists, who do not believe the Bible, think that all the plesiosaurs died out millions of years ago, before there was a man. But the Bible talks about God's work on Day 4 of Creation:

"And God said, Let the waters bring forth abundantly the moving creature that hath life,"
(Genesis 1:20).

This means that the swimming animals were made from the oceans just one day before God made man on Day 5. So, people lived with swimming animals like plesiosaurs since the very first week of creation. While on their boats, fisherman probably saw them in the sea. Maybe the plesiosaurs even swam close to land where people walking along the shore could see them.

Now Garth was not sure what to say. When he was thinking hard, his mustache curled up on the sides. He asked, "Does anybody tell stories about seeing giant

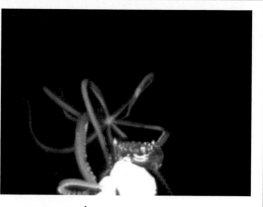

Giant Squid near Japan

Colossal Squid

sea monsters, like the stories of the monitor lizard in the Philippines?" Dino Dave told Garth about an animal called the giant squid. For many years, seamen brought back stories about huge squids as big as a boat that attacked their sailing ships. A few people tried to find this cryptid. However, most scientists did not believe in the giant squid. It seemed like just a crazy story! Then a dead giant squid washed onto the shore in Canada. In 2004 a live giant squid was seen on video near Japan. Japanese scientists took many photos. It was as big as a school bus and its eyes were as large as dinner plates. They even managed to rip off part of the squid's tentacle to prove that their pictures were real. Today we know that giant squids can grow to about 60 ft long and weigh as much as one ton. The stories of the old sailors were true after all!

Dino Dave said goodbye to his new friend Garth and went home. Awhile later, Dino Dave was reading the book of Ezekiel in his Bible. The prophet Ezekiel wrote about a scaly sea monster. This dragon swam up from the ocean into the big Nile River and stirred up the mud as it swam (Ezekiel 29:3-4). What kind of sea monster was this that would have been known in old Egypt? Dino Dave had seen a picture that the ancient Egyptians

had drawn, a picture of a kind of sea monster. It looks almost like the plesiosaurus. Egyptian fishermen catch fish with nets in the Nile River. The prophet Ezekiel talked about a sea dragon being caught in nets in the Nile River. The monster was pulled up onto the land to die (Ezekiel 32:2-3).

So, a plesiosaurus may have been seen alive in Egypt long ago. Some explorers today continue to report seeing new sea monsters. Two men went inside a small submarine called ALVIN (a special boat that travels deep underwater). They say they saw a living plesiosaur in a deep ocean trench. People who look for cryptids are

Egyptian Art   Plesiosaurus

called "cryptozoologists." These men and women try to find the hidden animals, especially in places where very few explorers have been, places like the deep ocean, wild jungles, or huge swamplands. A cryptozoologist looks for signs of the hidden animal, things like footprints, droppings, and bones from a skeleton or fur from a hide. Cryptozoologists talk to people to learn where the animal lives, what color it is, and when to find it.

Dino Dave is a cryptozoologist because he looks for dinosaurs that might still be alive today. He heard about a lady named Sandra who says she saw a plesiosaur in Lake Champlain in the state of Vermont. One warm July afternoon Sandra's family stopped on the shore of Lake Champlain near the town of St. Albans. Her children began to play in the lake water. Suddenly she saw something large moving out in the lake. At first, she thought it was a bunch of fish. But then a long neck came out of the water. It looked like a dinosaur. She took one photo and then watched as the monster disappeared underwater. This monster has been seen over many years, going all the way back to the explorer Samuel de Champlain who first discovered the lake.

Sandra's Champ photo

Searching Lake Champlain

Dino Dave decided to go to Vermont and look for Champ. He asked his friend Garth to come along too. It was a foggy day when they drove up the highway and through the Green Mountains. At last, they crossed a big bridge and there in front of them was the beautiful, deep Lake Champlain! For a long time, they looked out into the lake with binoculars, hoping to see Champ. Well, Dino Dave decided to stay a few days in a cabin on a small island. Early every morning he would look for Champ. He fished in the lake and went swimming.

He went on a big boat and crossed Lake Champlain to the state of New York. But he never saw Champ. Dino Dave talked with a lady named Katy. She has a special underwater microphone that lets her listen to sounds in the lake. One day Katy heard a strange sound that she thinks came from Champ. Dino Dave also found out about two fishermen who took a video of something with a long neck swimming near their boat. But it is hard to see if this is Champ.

Video of sea monster

After Garth heard all the stories about Champ, he believed that there was a plesiosaur still living in Lake Champlain. Even though many people say they have seen the lake monster, Champ is still hidden. We do not have a captured animal, like the big monitor lizard, or clear videos like the giant squid. So, we still call the monster the "Cryptid Champ." Proverbs 25:2 tells us that there is a glory in searching out and discovering hidden things. Maybe someday soon we will discover a living plesiosaur!

DINO DAVE'S QUESTIONS

1. What does the word cryptid mean? (A hidden animal)

2. What is the name of the man Dino Dave met who loves dinosaurs? (Garth)

3. God made the swimming creatures, like plesiosaurs, on what Day of Creation? (Day 5)

4. Were the scientists who said there were no giant squids right or wrong? (Wrong)

5. What lake is home to Champ? (Lake Champlain)

St. George & the Dragon
Crivelli, 1470

DINO DAVE & LA GRAND'GOULE

(Lesson: Historical accounts of people
fighting dragons fit with the Bible.)

What is this creature in the picture above? It looks like a fierce dragon! Its name is La Grand'Goule. That's a French name that means "the great monster." I'm going to tell you a story about this monster, a story that I think really happened about 500 years after Jesus lived. This dragon was first seen in the village of Poitiers in France. People said the monster lived in a deep, dark hole down in the swamps along the Clain River. At night it would fly out into the countryside to look for food to eat. It liked to eat little lambs, but sometimes it would even attack people! From the river, it would crawl up the water tunnels into the basements of houses to find something to eat. Then one day the monster came up into the cellar of the Sainte-Croix Abbey, a special church building in Poitiers. It killed one of the ladies living there. The people of the town decided that something had to be done about this terrible animal. Someone had to get a big, sharp sword and had to go down to the swamps where the city's water went into the river. They needed to hunt for the dragon until they found it and could kill it.

Ancient Town of Poitiers

Ah, but there was a problem. Everyone was scared! Who was willing to fight the monster? At last they talked to a prisoner who had been put in the town jail because he was very bad. They told him that he would be free if he would just go and fight La Grand'Goule. The man in prison agreed! He put on some armor, was given a long sword, and went down to the swamp. Finally, the brave prisoner was able to find the monster. There was a ferocious fight! When he returned to the village of Poitiers, the man's helmet was broken, and he was feeling faint and sick from the stinky breath of the monster.

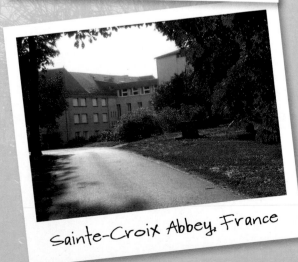

Sainte-Croix Abbey, France

17

La Grand'Goule parade

The dragon had tried to bite him, but the prisoner had won; and his sword had killed La Grand'Goule. The townspeople were so happy! They took the dead monster and carried it through the city in a big parade. The picture, drawn hundreds of years ago, shows their celebration. Every summer after that, there was a parade through the city of Poitiers to remember the killing of the dragon. In the year 1677, the women of the Sainte-Croix Abbey paid a carpenter to make a large wooden statue of the dragon. The dragon statue was carried through the city as part of the La Grand'Goule parade. Today, this beautiful dragon carving is kept safely in the Sainte-Croix Museum. This story of the killing of La Grand'Goule was written down by Sir John Lauder, a man from Scotland who lived in Poitiers in the 1600s.

How many of you girls and boys have heard stories like this about a big fierce dragon? Sometimes those stories are made up. They are fun to read about, but they are not always true. But there are times that we have stories about dragons that were very carefully written down in a book because the people say these things really happened. That's the way it is with the story of La Grand'Goule. The French wood carving of La Grand'Goule looks a lot like a flying reptile called Dimorphodon, a type of pterosaur. Each has wings like a bat and claws that come out at the edge of the wings. Both have a small head crest that sticks up behind the eyes. The dragon and the pterosaurs have strong hind legs and a long tail with a widening at the end (called a tail vane). How could the people of Poitiers have known what a Dimorphodon looked like when scientists did not discover its fossilized bones till hundreds of years later? It seems as if a large pterosaur was still living in France and was given the name La Grand'Goule, the great monster.

La Grand'Goule

Dimorphodon

The Bible also tells of dragons and how they lived near water (Ezekiel 29:3). Jeremiah 51:34 talks about a fierce king who led his army to conquer and destroy many people. It says,

18

"Nebuchadrezzar the king of Babylon hath devoured me, he hath crushed me...he hath swallowed me up like a dragon."

This verse reminds us of the way that large reptiles gulp up animals whole when they eat them. The prophets of God said that the city of Jerusalem would be broken down by King Nebuchadnezzar because of their disobedience to God. After that, King Nebuchadnezzar came with his armies and destroyed Jerusalem, just as the prophets said. The walls were broken down and the buildings were burned with fire. For a long time, the city was in ruins with nobody living there.

Jerusalem broken down

Finally, a man named Nehemiah was given permission to rebuild the walls of old Jerusalem. He traveled for many days on a horse to see what had happened to the great city. When he arrived to look at the broken-down city, the Bible says he came to a well that was called the "Dragon Well" (Nehemiah 2:13). Why did it have this name? Perhaps the broken-down walls near this wet place had become the home where a dragon lived. After killing or chasing off the dragon from its den, the people could again use this place for a well to get water. Then afterwards it was called the "Dragon Well." Look at the picture of the place people believe was the "Dragon Well" in the city of Jerusalem.

Jerusalem's dragon well

Some people who do not believe that the Bible is true just laugh at the stories of dragons in the Bible. They say that dragons are just "make believe." But carefully written stories from countries all around the continent of Europe help us to understand that there were dragons living in many places long after the Bible was completed. Dino Dave heard about more dragon stories like La Grand'Goule that came from old Europe, hundreds of years ago, a time we call the Middle Ages. Dino Dave traveled around Europe to learn about some of these dragon stories.

He traveled to a place in the country of Hungary where a dragon was killed. Dino Dave also read a story named Beowulf, written in the country of England. It told about a hero who liked to travel around and fight dragons. The story of Beowulf was written about 900 AD. It is a very famous book in England. Dino Dave heard about a place in Poland where a dragon lived in 700 AD. The dragon made its home in a large cave on the side of the Vistula River. A man named Skuba killed the dragon, and the people living there say its bones were hung in Wawel Cathedral, the town's church. There are big bones still hanging in the church to this day.

Dino Dave & Hungarian dragon

In the 1500s, in the country of Italy, there lived a famous scientist named Aldrovandus. He was very smart and taught many students. Aldrovandus collected thousands of animals and plants to make the first-ever natural history museum. One of the animals in his museum was a dragon. Aldrovandus carefully wrote down how the dragon was discovered on May 13, 1572. At 5:00 PM in the evening a man

Wawel Cathedral bones

named Baptista was driving his oxen down a dirt road. Suddenly the oxen stopped and would not move forward. Baptista kicked them and shouted at them, but they refused to move. Then he heard a strange hissing sound and looked up the road in front of the oxen. He was very surprised to see a strange little dragon on the road. Baptista took a big stick and hit the small dragon on the head and killed it. Then he gave the dead dragon to the scientist Aldrovandus. So Aldrovandus carefully studied the dead animal. He decided that the little dragon was a baby, because of its small claws and teeth. It had only two feet and so he thought that it moved partly by slithering like a snake and partly by pushing with its feet. Aldrovandus stuffed the dragon and put it into his museum. He also had a painting of the dragon made.

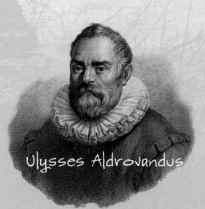

Ulysses Aldrovandus

Dragons were scary creatures that were sometimes very fierce and could even kill people. But the Bible makes an amazing promise to

people that love God. It says in Psalm 91:13 "the dragon shalt thou trample under feet." We know from stories in history that people have killed dragons and have stepped on top of the dead dragon in triumph. The Bible is exactly right. We have lots of dragon stories and even many drawings of people killing dragons. On page 16, you can see a famous painting of St. George killing a flying dragon. It looks almost like La Grand'Goule! How can a fighting man beat a dragon? Being prepared and well-armed with a sharp weapon is important. But trusting in God to help is even more important. Proverbs 21:31 says,

"The horse is prepared against the day of battle: but safety is of the LORD."

Do you want safety and victory in your life? Learn to love and trust God. Then you don't have to be afraid, even of a dragon!

DINO DAVE'S QUESTIONS

1. What does the French name "La Grand'Goule" mean? (The great monster)

2. The French wood carving looks a lot like what reptile? (A Dimorphodon pterosaur)

3. Who was the man who came to rebuild Jerusalem's walls and traveled to the Dragon Well? (Nehemiah)

4. Where did the scientist Aldrovandus keep the stuffed, dead dragon? (In his museum)

5. What does the Bible say will be trampled under the feet of those who trust God? (Dragons)

ADVENTURE 3

DINO DAVE & RATIONALIST RICK

(Lesson: Biblical faith is a strong, reasonable foundation for life.)

Dino Dave was working on a big project at his house. He was building a new garage. Many people came to help. First a man with a big machine, called an excavator, came to prepare the ground for the garage. He was very kind and let Dino Dave's son drive the machine. How exciting! After all the digging in the ground, concrete was poured in a big square to make the garage's foundation. Starting with a good foundation is one of the most important parts of proper building. The foundation supports everything else! Next, carpenters came to help build the new garage

Driving the excavator

with big wood boards. That is when Dino Dave first met Rick. That summer, they became friends. Dino Dave began to pray for an opportunity to talk to his new friend about the good news in the Bible.

The garage walls were starting to go up and the building began to look like a garage. "Once the walls and roof are done," Rick explained, "a special truck will come and help us finish the bottom floor." After another day the roof was almost complete. Rick told Dino Dave, "Tomorrow the special truck will come." Do any of you children know what kind of a truck Rick meant? The next morning a

Garage foundation

Garage walls

Garage roof

Pouring concrete

cement truck drove up. It poured the concrete floor for the new garage. A man worked to smooth out the concrete so that the floor would be nice and even. Concrete looks kind of like mud, but it is strong and heavy because it contains ground up rocks and cement (see the page background). When it dries, it becomes as hard as a rock.

That morning, Dino Dave was reading Hebrews chapter 11 in the Bible. He told Rick about some of the things he learned, stories about the wonderful miracles God did for people that had faith in Him. But Rick did not believe those Bible stories. He thought having faith in God was silly. Rick said that he only believed in things he could see and understand with his mind. Rick was a rationalist. Rationalists believe that human reasoning is the only way of knowing things. They do not believe in things that they can't completely understand, things like the miracles in the Bible.

Dino Dave & Rationalist Rick

Dino Dave asked Rick, "Have you seen the country of Cambodia? Do you completely understand electricity?" Dino Dave explained that there are a lot of things we believe and use every day, even though we can't see them or completely understand them. Every one of us uses faith every day. Faith is not bad. It is just believing something that you have not seen or tested. Rationalist Rick asked, "But how can you believe in miracles? They're impossible!" Dino Dave explained that if God made the whole universe, it would be easy for Him to show His power at special times by doing a miracle. Most of the time, He lets His universe run by the natural laws that He made. But He can also break those laws. That should not surprise us, even if we cannot understand how He worked the miracle.

Faith in the Bible is a reasonable belief. It does make sense. It is based on something we call evidence, which is facts that support it. Hebrews 11:1 teaches,

"Now faith is the substance of things hoped for, the *evidence* of things not seen."

Dino Dave explaining faith

Our faith is very firm, based on us seeing how God keeps His promises. It is faith because we cannot see God or Heaven, but it does fit with what we see. Faith in the God of the Bible is very reasonable. We may not understand everything about God. He is bigger than we are, and His thoughts are higher than our thoughts (Isaiah 55:8-9). So, it should not bother us that we can't completely understand Him. That is when we need to trust in what the Bible says about Him.

Rationalist Rick did not want to trust the Bible. He only trusted his own mind to understand things. Boys and girls, have you ever changed your mind? Of course! We are always learning new things. Can one of you children share how you changed your mind recently? So, believing only what we completely understand is not a solid foundation for our life. We know how easily our minds can change! "Rick," said Dino Dave, "How can you build your life without God? If there is no God who created us, there is no reason to expect our mind to even work right. If everything is just an accident, there should be no purpose and no truth. We could not even trust our own thinking to lead us correctly!" This made sense to Rationalist Rick and he nodded. But then he had to get back to working.

Dino Dave's garage was getting quickly built, day by day. On the top of the roof, there was going to be a special little part of the building to let in light and air. It is called a cupola. The workers used tall ladders going up the

Building the cupola

Finished garage

back of the garage to put the cupola on top. Finally, the garage was finished! Dino Dave was able to move many important things into the garage: his family's bikes, his tractor, his research tools, and his dinosaur things. Dino Dave has many dinosaur fossils, dinosaur books, and even a dinosaur costume. The dinosaur costume is huge and takes up a lot of space. Rationalist Rick helped Dino Dave move the costume into the garage and hang it in place.

"How does this dinosaur costume work?" asked Rick. Dino Dave explained that a person climbs inside of it and walks around. There are buttons to make the dinosaur blink its eyes, open its mouth, and roar loudly! Because the costume can move like a real dinosaur, it is called an animatronic dinosaur. It is shaped like a very fierce, meat-eating Carnotaurus.

Inside the garage

Animatronic dinosaur

Dino Dave likes to take this dinosaur into the city. Children come running to see the dinosaur. Then Dino Dave tells their whole family about how God made the dinosaurs and all the things in this world. God created every boy and girl to have a special purpose. He gave us a mind and wants us to think about Him, read His Word and know Him. God says,

"Come now, and let us reason together, saith the Lord: though your sins be as scarlet, they shall be as white as snow;" (Isaiah 1:18).

Dino Dave gives people little papers called tracts that tell them the facts about Jesus.

Dino Dave's finished garage is good-looking on the outside. But the important thing is that many special items have a safe, dry place in which to stay. The garage is strong because it was built on a solid concrete foundation. Jesus once told a story about two people who were building houses. A wise man found a large rock cliff, and he built his house on the stone. The foolish man saw how much work it was to carry all the wood up the cliff. He decided to build his house in an easier place, right on a sandy beach. Then Jesus said that a big storm came. The wind blew hard, and the rain came pouring down. It began to wash away the sand. What do you think happened to the house on the sand? The foolish man's house was destroyed. But the house built on the rock stood firm.

Building on the rock

Building on the sand

The storm comes

Jesus told this story so that we would think about the foundation of our lives. He said that whosoever obeys His commands is like the wise man who built his house upon the rock (Matthew 7:24). Some people build their lives on the foundation of what is popular, what other people around them are thinking. But popular ideas come and go. Many great kingdoms have been destroyed and what their

people believed is gone too. The Bible makes the best authority on which to build our lives. It is like the concrete that is the foundation for Dino Dave's garage. Some people build their life by only believing in human reasoning. The foundation of their life is like sand. Children, will you make your life's foundation of sand, like Rationalist Rick? Or will you build your foundation on the rock of Jesus Christ? The foundation of a building doesn't seem that important. Sometimes, it is hard to even see it because it is in the ground. But the foundation is very important! When the storms of life come, the foundation you build as a young person will decide how strong the rest of your life will be.

Dino Dave's Questions

1. What did Dino Dave build at his house? (A new garage)

2. What was used to make the foundation for the new garage? (Concrete)

3. What do we call someone who believes that human reasoning is the only way of knowing things? (A rationalist)

4. Where did the foolish man in the story Jesus told build his house? (On a sandy beach)

5. What can we do to build our life on a good foundation? (Believe the Bible and obey the commands of Jesus)

ADVENTURE 4

DINO DAVE & THE COMPLICATED CELL

(Lesson: Cells in living things are complex and point to an intelligent Creator.)

Boys and girls, did you know that long before you became as big as you are, you started out as something very, very small. I'm not just talking about when you were a baby. I want to talk about when each of you started out as something so small that it couldn't even be seen with our eyes. You started out as a single speck that looked like the blue circle at the top of the page. This is a single human cell. It has been made bigger in this picture so we can see it. Even though it is tiny, it is made of so many parts that it is hard for us to understand how it works. We say the cell is very complicated.

Every person, even you, started out life as a single cell. Then the cell began to split in half to make 2 cells stuck together. Then those 2 divided to make 4, then 8, next 16, and then many cells. Then these many cells began to make special body parts that we call tissue, like skin tissue and bone tissue, that make up your body. After that, you grew into a little baby. A human baby has 26 trillion cells! The most basic working part of every single living thing in the world is the cell. Cells are amazing! Today I want to talk to you a little bit about what we can learn from studying cells.

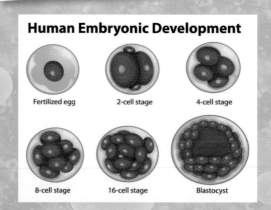

Every baby started as a single cell

When Dino Dave was younger, he began to think about an important question. He wondered: "What does it mean to be alive?" He began to make a list of ways we can know something is alive.

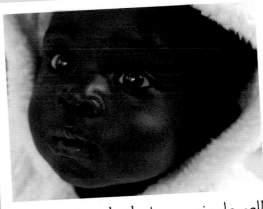

Human Embryonic Development

Fertilized egg   2-cell stage   4-cell stage

8-cell stage   16-cell stage   Blastocyst

alive   not alive

Look at this picture and see if you can tell what is alive and what is not alive. OK, what are some things that living creatures do that non-living things like stones or toy dinosaurs do not do? Living things breathe, eat, grow and change. They respond to other things and can usually move. This list helps us to understand what is alive. Some living creatures are so tiny that their whole body is just one cell. To the right is a picture of some single-celled bacteria. They may be little, but they are still alive. They eat and move and respond to things around them. They can multiply so that there are more and more bacteria. From the tiniest living thing to the biggest living thing, they all are made of cells.

Young Dino Dave

After Dino Dave learned as a young boy what it was to be alive, he had another question. Where did the first living cell come from? Do any of you children know the answer to that question? The Bible gives us the answer in Acts 17:25

"He [God] giveth to all life, and breath, and all things."

God, with His amazing knowledge and wisdom is the Creator of all the beautiful living things.

But people used to believe that living cells could just all of a sudden come from dead things. People saw that if you left out food (like maybe some old soup), it would get mold on it. The mold is a living thing that people once thought came right up out of the non-living soup. Dino Dave heard about a man who lived in the country of France. This man was a Christian, and he believed the Bible. He did not think it was correct that living cells all by themselves could come out of non-living things like soup. This man's name was Louis Pasteur.

Louis had a different idea about where mold came from. He thought that maybe there were teeny, tiny mold cells floating in the air. They could land on things like the soup and start to multiply: first 1 cell, then 2 cells, then 4 cells until pretty soon you could see a lot of mold growing in the soup. As the mold began to eat the soup, it would grow until the soup was moldy all over.

Soup jar experiment

Louis Pasteur decided to test his idea with an experiment. He made some soup and cooked it so hot that any tiny living cells that might be floating in the soup were killed. Everything in there was dead. Then he took half of the soup and poured it into a container and made it so dust could *not* come in. The other half he took and poured into a container and left it open to the air where dust and tiny things floating in the air *could* fall in. Then he waited to see what would happen. Well, guess what happened in this famous experiment? The container that was left open to the air grew mold, just like the soup shown in this jar on the right of the picture. But the container that did not allow the air to drop dust in did not grow mold, just like the soup on the left of the picture. The Louis Pasteur experiment showed that living things like mold cannot come from dead things like soup. It takes a living cell to come in the air and drop into the soup to begin to grow a lot of mold as you see in the picture.

Because of Louis Pasteur's work, scientists now know that life only comes from other things that are alive. In science we have important rules called laws. Science laws tell us how things will happen in the world. One of the laws that is now very famous is called the Law of Biogenesis. Now that's an awfully big word, but it simply means that "Life only comes from life!" Because Louis Pasteur helped us to understand this truth, he became very famous. His idea of how to make food last longer and not get moldy is still used today. In this picture you see some *Pasteurized* milk. This heating and sealing process for food is called *Pasteurization*. The name *Pasteurization* came from the work of the amazing Christian man, Louis Pasteur.

But some people who do not know or do not believe the Bible still think that the first life came on this earth all by itself, just from rocks and water. Why do they want to believe this, even though the Law of Biogenesis says that it couldn't happen? Because if life only comes from life, then there must be a God who was alive and made the first life on this Earth. These people do *not* want to believe in God. How sad! The Bible tells us,

"The fool hath said in his heart, There is no God" (Psalm 14:1).

When we study the cell, it helps us see just how smart our God is to create it. The smartest scientists in the world cannot make a cell in their laboratory. It is too complicated. The cell has lots of special pieces and parts to it, and it has lots of amazing "machines" in it that make it work. Before we had microscopes to be able to see a cell, scientists used to think that maybe the cell was just like a tiny bag of some goo. They could see the outside of the cell but not all the stuff on the inside. Then scientists began to learn more and could see the cell's inside. They decided it was more like a building with lots of rooms in it. Now we know that the cell is full of containers with complicated machines. It is more like a city that has a wall around it with special gates to let certain things in and out. It has lots of

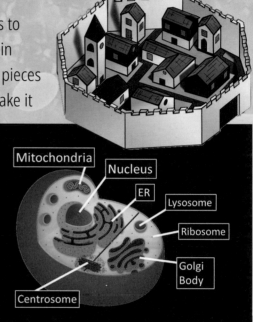

traffic moving down special roads. There are different areas that are much like the buildings of a city: a library, a post office, a police department, an energy plant, a factory, and much more. Children, do you think a city like that could come together all by itself without anyone building it? No, it takes a great deal of planning and hard work to build a whole town that is secure and works well.

The more scientists study the cell, the more we see how carefully it had to be put together. It has so many tiny parts and is so complicated. All the parts do important things, kind of like all the tiny parts of a beautiful pocket watch. If we just decided to take some parts *out* of the watch, guess what would happen? The watch would not work right. All these parts must be there in the right place at the same time or it will be broken and won't do its job. It is the same for the complicated cell. If all the important parts of a cell were not there, the cell would die.

Here is a picture of Dino Dave holding a bunch of watch parts. Do you think that these parts could come together by themselves without a watchmaker? No! It would be crazy to believe that.

Louis Pasteur once said, "The more I study nature, the more I stand amazed at the work of the Creator." The tiny cell is certainly an amazing part of the Creator's work. The Bible says in Romans 1:20,

Dino Dave & DNA with watch parts

> **"For the invisible things of him [God] from the creation of the world are clearly seen, being understood by the things that are made".**

The more we study even tiny living things, like the complicated cell, the more we see that we have a very smart God!

DINO DAVE'S QUESTIONS

1. Is every living thing made of a cell or many cells? (Yes)

2. What are some of the ways we know if something is alive? (It may breathe, eat, grow, change, respond, or move.)

3. Did Louis Pasteur believe living mold could come from dead things? (No)

4. What is the name of the law in science that says life only comes from life? (The Law of Biogenesis)

5. Who made the first complicated cell? (God)

DINO DAVE & FOSSIL FUELS

(Lesson: The fuels formed from living things are from the great Genesis Flood.)

One day Dino Dave was driving down the road and suddenly he saw a gas station that had a very special sign, a sign that said the name *Sinclair* and showed a big green dinosaur! Well, Dino Dave loves dinosaurs, and so he hit the brakes and quickly stopped the car so that he could see this special fuel station. There was even a big green dinosaur by the parking lot! A man came over to help fill Dino Dave's car with gasoline. When the car's tank was full of gas, Dino Dave asked the man working there why they had put a green dinosaur on their sign. The man said, "Don't you know? Gasoline comes from dead dinosaurs that were buried in the earth millions and millions of years ago!" The man thanked Dino Dave for buying some fuel and then went back to his work.

Dino Dave does not believe that the dinosaurs lived millions of years ago. But as he drove down the road, Dino Dave began thinking that maybe he should learn more about fuel. He knew that gasoline starts out as something called oil that is taken from the ground.

The Sinclair dinosaur

Thick, black oil oozing out of the ground was first seen many years ago. Even the Bible talks about it. The book of Exodus records the true story of when Moses was a baby. The Bible says that Moses' mom put him in a little boat, like a basket, and placed it in the Nile River. But she did something special so that it would float well. She got some pitch, like a very thick oil.

pitch on bottom

The Bible says she took her little boat and she

"daubed it with slime and with pitch, and put the child therein;" (Exodus 2:3).

She "daubed it," means that she spread the oily pitch onto the bottom of the little boat to seal it so that no water could get in. Pretty soon the pitch hardened, almost like the tar of a road. Oil does not mix with water. So, it is good for making things waterproof. People living in old Egypt knew that placing tar on the outside of a boat would make it strong and keep it dry inside. But how does this oil coming up from the ground get turned into gasoline?

Dino Dave & Geologist John

Dino Dave decided to talk with a scientist named John who worked with the Earth's rock layers that contain oil. This type of scientist is called a geologist. Dino Dave traveled to the big state of Texas where there is lots of oil that comes from the ground. He visited with Geologist John and asked him about gasoline. Geologist John explained how the fuel companies find oil under the ground, and how they get a big drilling machine to dig down through the rocks to where the oil is located. Then they put a pipe into the hole that they made. Next, a pump is put in place so that the oil can be pushed up and out. Oil pumps like this work all day and all night...going up and down, up and down, up and down. Some pumps have been working like this for fifty years! When oil first comes out of the ground, it is black and very gooey. It is stored in big metal tanks. Then an oil truck comes to take it to a special place called a refinery.

Oil digging rig

Grasshopper oil pump

Inside oil refinery

Sinclair oil truck

When the oil arrives at a refinery, it goes through many pipes and filters. The refineries boil the oil and add things to it so that it will not be so black and gooey. Afterwards, it is changed to clear gasoline that looks almost like water. Next the gasoline is stored in huge round tanks. Then the oil companies use big tanker trucks to deliver the finished gasoline to the fuel stations where people can put the gas into their cars. Maybe this tanker in the picture is bringing gas to a station with a dinosaur, much like the one where Dino Dave stopped to get gas.

Dino Dave at Sinclair Station

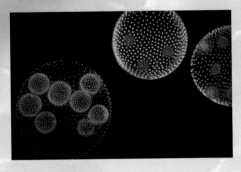

Dino Dave asked Geologist John if oil really came from dead dinosaurs. John laughed. "No, that's what some people used to think. But now we know that oil is *not* from dead dinosaurs." John explained that oil mostly came from tiny sea life like plants. That's why much of the oil is found below the bottom of the oceans. Oil started out as living things called bacteria, plankton and algae. Do you see the picture of the beautiful single-celled algae? It is so small that we must look at it through a microscope. So, oil is really fossilized ocean life. Another important fossil fuel is coal. Earth's coal started as trees, ferns, and other forest plants that lived in a warm place. That's why the coal is usually found on land. Both oil and coal are called "fossil fuels." They are the leftovers or "fossils" of things like plants that lived in the past.

Then Dino Dave asked Geologist John about the idea that it took millions of years for the oil to form down under the earth. John told Dino Dave about an experiment that government scientists did. Since oil comes mostly from algae, scientists decided to try to make oil out of today's ocean algae. They found that it can form very quickly. In 2013, government scientists reported that they were able to change algae into oil in less than one hour! It doesn't take millions of years. It just takes the right conditions, including lots of heat and pressure.

Algae turned into oil

Those exact conditions would have happened during the great Genesis Flood that we read about in the Bible. Tons of hot water came up out of the ground. Genesis 7:11 says that "all the fountains of the great deep were broken up." Then, the water that covered the whole Earth (II Peter 3:6) would have pushed down and made great pressure. As a result, untold numbers of plants and sea organisms would have been buried and turned into fossil fuel.

But Geologist John told Dino Dave something else. When the oil companies use a drill to start digging a hole deep down to get to the oil, sometimes they find that the oil is *still* under a lot of pressure. It comes squirting up to the surface in a fountain. In the picture you can see an oil fountain gushing up. One oil well in Texas gushed more than 4,200,000 gallons of oil per day and made an oil fountain 200 feet up into the air! Geologist John explained that oil under so much pressure should have oozed out through the rocks to the surface if the oil had been there for millions of years. Oil that is still under great pressure tells us that the oil has not been there for millions of years.

oil well gushing

Natural gas is another fossil fuel. Because it is like air, it should have leaked out of the ground even easier than oil. In fact, natural gas is lighter than the air that we breathe, and so it wants to fly up into the sky. But when natural gas is found today, it's still under great pressure down in the rocks. Two thousand years ago, the Chinese used the pressure of natural gas that they had discovered under the ground in China. They made pipes out of bamboo and channeled the gas into their homes where it provided heat and light.

In the 1930s, one of the directors of Standard Oil Company read the story in Exodus 2:3 about Moses' mom making a little boat covered with "slime and pitch." He believed that the stories in the Bible were completely true. And he knew that if oily pitch had been leaking out from the ground, there must be some oil buried there in Egypt. So, he sent the company geologist to look for oil there. The discovery of oil in Egypt led to Standard Oil Company having many oil wells both on land and in the ocean around Egypt.

Oil in Egypt

Dino Dave learned that fossil fuels like oil, coal and natural gas do not come from dead dinosaurs. They come from dead plants and sea life. These fuels can form very quickly in conditions exactly like those that happened during the Genesis Flood. It does not take millions of years. In fact, the pressure in the oil and gas wells tells us that it has *not* been millions of years. These fossil fuels come from the Genesis Flood just thousands of years ago. When we believe the stories in the Bible, they help us to understand the world around us today, just as they helped the Director of Standard Oil to find oil in Egypt. We can believe everything that the Bible says because it is God's Word! Will you, young people, grow up to believe God's Word and let it guide you? Psalm 119:105 says,

"Thy word is a lamp unto my feet, and a light unto my path."

DINO DAVE'S QUESTIONS

1. Does gasoline come from dead dinosaurs?
   (No, it comes from dead sea life.)

2. Who was the baby in the Bible who was put into a little boat in the Nile River? (Moses)

3. What is the name of the place that turns oil into gasoline?
   (A refinery)

4. What can we learn from oil and natural gas being under pressure?
   (It has not been there millions of years.)

5. How did the Director of Standard Oil know to look for oil in Egypt? (By reading the Bible)

DINO DAVE & THE LAVA LAYERS

(Lesson: Studying lava layers forming today teaches
us that Earth's rock layers formed quickly.)

Volcanoes are very, very scary. They happen when the really hot, melted rock from deep inside the Earth is squeezed up onto the surface of the world where we live. When the hot red, melted rock goo comes squirting out, it is called lava. How hot is the lava? It is between 1000 and 2000 degrees! That is so hot that it burns anything that it touches. Psalm 104:32 shows the greatness of our God when it says,

**"He looketh on the earth, and it trembleth:
he toucheth the hills, and they smoke."**

Volcanoes are usually big mountains. At the top of the mountain there is a hole that is the main lava tube or vent. At the bottom of the hole is the magma chamber full of melted rock. After the hot lava comes pouring out of the top of the vent, it flows down into the valleys just like a river; and then it begins to cool. The cold lava makes a layer of hard, black rock that looks like a paved highway. Dino Dave wanted to learn more about volcanic rocks, and so he decided to visit the largest active volcano on Earth. This volcano, called Mauna Loa, is on the island of Hawaii.

Testing red hot lava

Lava coming from Mauna Loa sometimes flows right down into the ocean. While Dino Dave was there, he could see the big clouds of steam coming from that very hot lava flowing into the sea. But the lava also covered the land with a layer up to 30 feet thick. Even some of the roads were covered! All the grasses, bushes and flowers living there were burned up by the hot lava.

Mauna Loa Volcano on Hawaii

Ants, spiders and other insects were covered and killed. All that was left was a thick, hard, black layer of rock. Not far away on the same island is another volcano called Kilauea. The lava from this volcano caused even more damage by flowing very quickly near a village. The lava covered cars and even started houses on fire! Seven hundred homes were destroyed. Truly a volcano is a scary thing. It shows us how small we are and how great our God is to have control over the whole world. Psalm 97:5 says,

"The mountains melt like wax at the presence of the Lord..."

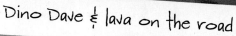

Dino Dave & lava on the road

After the thick lava layer cools into cold rock, no plants grow in that area for a long time. It is a wasteland of bare, black, hard rock with no animals living there. But after a while, something interesting starts to happen. The wind and rain start to knock little bits off the black lava stone,

Kilauea flowing over the road

to make tiny pieces of black sand. This is called erosion. Sometimes, when it rains for many days, pools of water form. Then the water starts to flow like a brook over the lava layers. Flowing water begins to dig into the hard rock layer. Soon, cracks appear in the rocks and little seeds blown into the cracks by the wind start to grow, digging their roots into the cracks and sand and causing more erosion. Look at the top of the next page. Can you see the picture of small plants starting to grow in the cracks of a black lava layer in Hawaii?

Next, small animals start to return to the area. Tiny ants and spiders begin to build homes in the rock. After that, lizards and toads come along to eat those small insects that are living there. Notice on the next page a picture of a small Lava Lizard that likes to make its home on the black volcanic layers in Hawaii.

Lava layer being eroded

Not long after that, bushes will begin growing where once there was only hard black rock. Then larger animals start to come back, like rabbits and gophers. Here is a picture of a pocket gopher looking out of its black volcanic sand home. By digging to make their burrows, gophers stir up the ground. This mixes the lava layer with some of the lower layers. Next, the trees start to grow again and then you would never know that there had been such a big layer of lava everywhere. In Hawaii, this whole process from hard black lava to a new forest has taken place in just 65 years!

But sometimes volcanoes don't just push out lava. Here is a picture of Mount St. Helens, a volcano that erupted or exploded in the state of Washington in 1980. It made a big mess over 20,000 square miles with lots of ash, dust, hot gases and a type of lava called pumice. In the picture, you can see Dino Dave holding a handful of ash that came from Mount St. Helens. Because

Mount St. Helens eruption

the hot ash covered the land, it killed all the living things on the surface. One area to the north of the volcano, called the Pumice Plain, is 6-square-miles that was buried under 13 feet of 1200 degree volcanic ash! But scientists were very surprised at how fast living plants came back to these ash layers. Just 35 years later, the Pumice Plain is now a beautiful meadowland.

Pumice Plain 1985

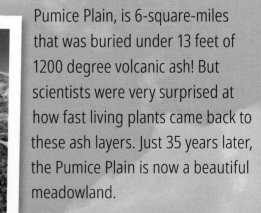

Mt. St. Helens Pumice Plain 2015

There are other natural disasters that leave large layers on the land. Big floods can leave behind a large layer of mud or sand. A huge wave, called a tsunami can also carry lots of mud up onto land. These layers can then harden, almost like concrete. But they are usually not as hard as a lava rock layer. Sometimes landslides (dirt and rock that falls down the sides of a mountain) can leave a big messy layer that covers the ground. But since mud and sand layers are usually softer than lava layers, they turn back into fields and forests even more quickly than what happened in Hawaii and at Mount St. Helens.

2015 mudflow in Brazil

Studying lava layers taught Dino Dave an important lesson about the rock layers that we see in the ground. Look at these beautiful rock layers forming the hillside in the picture. How long do you think it took for all those layers to form? Well, if a lower layer was left alone on the surface for hundreds or thousands of years before the next layer covered it, it would begin to turn back to forest. There would be marks of erosion (like cracking and loose sand), brooks that flowed, roots of bushes and trees and animal burrows. Look carefully. Do you see signs of these kinds of activities between these rock layers? No, there is only a layer of rock...and then right away another layer of rock on top of it. They are just like layers of a yummy birthday cake. Each one is stacked tightly on top of the other. There are no holes that animals have dug or streams that have been buried. This tells us that the next layer came quickly after the one under it was spread out. Each layer was covered before there was time to disturb the bottom layer.

Tightly stacked rock layers

The Bible helps us to understand what happened on Earth many years ago. Psalm 104 talks about the great Flood of Genesis. Verse 6 says, "the waters stood above the mountains." Waves that were so big that they could cover mountains brought layer after layer of mud and sand up onto the land. There were also a lot of volcanoes at that time. There were *many* lava layers formed. The Genesis Flood explains how huge rock layers that cover large parts of the world were made very quickly...one on top of the other. When we look at the lava layers that are formed today, we understand how the big rock layers from the past must have happened. It did not happen slowly over millions of years.

After teaching about the Flood, Psalm 104 reminds us that God will never again destroy the Earth with water. He gave us the rainbow as a sign of this promise. Psalm 104 goes on to describe how the Lord waters the valleys and gives grass for the cattle and trees where birds can live. He gives grains from the ground so that we can make bread to feed ourselves. After the great Flood, God allowed the Earth to quickly recover from the catastrophe, just like the way that we see it recover from volcanoes still today. This is part of His goodness, and we should thank Him for it.

Rainbow over Bryce Canyon

"Oh that men would praise the LORD for his goodness, and for his wonderful works!" (Psalm 107:31).

Dino Dave's Questions

1. The huge volcano Mauna Loa is in what state? (Hawaii)

2. What is it called when wind and rain start to knock little bits off the black lava stone, making tiny pieces of black sand? (Erosion)

3. Does it take millions of years for plants to grow and for animals to dig in the lava layers? (No, it happened in 65 years.)

4. When we look at Earth's rock layers, do we usually see signs of animal and plant activity in the layers? (No)

5. The Bible helps us understand that the rock layers were formed very quickly during what large catastrophe? (The Flood)

ADVENTURE 7

DINO DAVE & THE MIDNIGHT MOON

(Lesson: A close look at the Moon
teaches us about its wonderful design.)

Do you see that big grey ball at the top of the page? What is that? That's the Moon. When we see it at night, it looks so bright and far away. We can't see all of its details. But that's how it looks if you are up close to it. Dino Dave's friend Garth likes studying the Moon. "Hey Dino Dave," he said one afternoon, "Do you want to stay up late with me tonight and see the *supermoon*?" Dino Dave asked him what a supermoon was. Garth said, "It's when the Moon looks really big because it's close to the Earth as it travels through space." He explained to Dino Dave that this supermoon would look 15% brighter than a normal full moon. The best time to look at the moon would be midnight. Well, Dino Dave wanted to see the supermoon. So, he took his doggie, DNA, and they went to visit his friend Garth. DNA helped to drive along the way. When they arrived, the Moon was rising, and they found Garth already looking through a long tube that pointed up into the sky. Do any of you children know what we call this special looking machine with the long tube? It is called a telescope.

DNA helping to drive

The telescope is a wonderful machine because it lets us see objects from Earth that we cannot go out into space and look at closely. The first person who made a telescope to look up at the sky was an Italian man named Galileo. At that time, scientists thought the Moon was just a big, smooth ball. Galileo looked through the telescope and found that the Moon has mountains and valleys, much like the Earth. Galileo was also able to learn about other planets and their moons.

Garth and his telescope

Then they opened the door of the Lunar Module and climbed down the ladder. For the first time, people walked on the Moon! For two hours Neil and Buzz explored the surroundings. Their space suits helped them to survive by keeping them warm and giving them oxygen to breathe. They dug up 47 pounds of Moon dirt to be studied on the Earth. Then they climbed back into the Lunar Module and took off from the Moon's surface and returned to their rocket. From the rocket, Steve saw them and took a picture with the Earth rising behind them. Once all three astronauts were again on board, the rocket returned to Earth. It splashed down safely into the Pacific Ocean on July 24. After eight days in space, they were finally back home. A helicopter picked up the three astronauts from the ocean and took them to a navy ship that was waiting for them. After that, there was a big celebration!

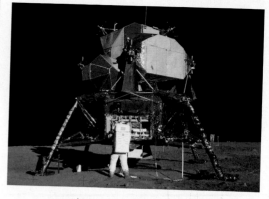

Apollo II Lunar Module

Apollo II Pacific Ocean landing

While Dino Dave was visiting the space center, there was a rocket that launched into the sky with a loud roar that shook the buildings. Dino Dave was able to put on a space suite and meet with an astronaut to ask questions. The astronaut explained that the Moon does some important things for us on Earth. The Moon's orbit allowed people long ago to develop a calendar with months. Every time that the Moon circled around the Earth, the ancient people called it one month. This helped them to mark off the seasons so that they knew when it would be springtime and when the winter would come. This was God's plan. The Bible says, "He appointed the moon for seasons:" (Psalm 104:19).

Our Moon also makes it nicer to live on the Earth because it helps with our weather. The Earth pulls on the Moon as it spins around. That's what keeps it from flying out into space. It is like swinging a string with a ball around your head. As long as you hold onto the string, the ball keeps going around and around. But if you let go, the ball will fly off. The Earth's pull on the Moon is called gravity. But the Moon also pulls back on the Earth (like the ball pulls on your hand). The Moon's pull causes the water of the oceans to rise and fall, which is called tides. The tides help to remove bad things from the seashore, and they also move bits of food into shore so that ocean plants and animals can live.

Moon's Orbit

Some scientists do not think that God made the Moon. They think that 4 billion years ago a big meteor smashed into the world, causing a chunk of earth to go flying off into space to become the Moon. Do you remember how we said that the Moon is like a ball on a string that you spin around your head? What happens if you let go of the string? That's right. The ball will go flying away from you. Well, the Earth's gravity is slowly letting go of the Moon. Every year the Moon moves a couple of inches further out from the Earth. This means that the Moon should be a lot further out if it had really been 4 billion years since its creation. No, the Moon's orbit fits with what the Bible says. God, the Creator, made our wonderful Moon thousands of years ago, not billions, and it shows us His great design.

DINO DAVE'S QUESTIONS

1. Did the Supermoon look twice as big as a normal full Moon? (No, it was only 15% brighter than a normal full Moon.)

2. What is the machine that lets us see objects far out into space? (A telescope)

3. Which side of the Moon has more craters, the near side, or the far away side? (The far away side)

4. What was the name of the Christian man who was the second person to step onto the Moon? (Buzz Aldrin)

5. What can we learn from the Moon slowly moving away from the Earth? (The Moon is only thousands of years old.)

ADVENTURE 8

Dino Dave & the Bombardier Beetle

(Lesson: Fiery beetles and fiery dragons show
God's power and how we should fear Him.)

Dino Dave likes the big, fierce dinosaurs because they are exciting to study and learn about. But Dino Dave also loves some other very interesting animals that help us to understand the Bible better. Today, I want to tell you the story of a strange little creature that is still alive today. It isn't big and scary, like a dinosaur. It is not even as long as your thumb. It is a little orange and black beetle called the Bombardier Beetle. To learn why the Bombardier Beetle helps us to understand the Bible better, we need to tell the Bible story of Job.

Job is the oldest book in the Bible. It tells about a man named Job who loved God and did what was right. God blessed him with lots of farm animals. But one day some very terrible things happened to Job. Have you ever had really bad things happen to you? In one day, Job lost all his animals and even his family. Then he became sick with a disease called boils. The boils were big sores on his skin from the very top of his head all the way down to the very bottoms of his feet. Job was very sad and hurting so much that he began to question where God was, and whether God still cared about him. But then God came

and began to talk to Job. After that, Job understood more about God's great power and wisdom. Job learned that he could trust God, even in this very hard time of his life.

In chapter 41 of the book of Job, God told Job about a ferocious animal called Leviathan. The Bible says that it is one of the fiercest creatures that God made. We don't know exactly what this animal was. However, we do know that Leviathan lived in water.

It had tough scales on its skin, sharp teeth in its mouth, a strong neck and it could *breathe fire*. The Bible tells us that *a flame goes out of its mouth and sparks of fire come out when he breathes!* Out of his nose comes smoke. (Job 41:19-21) Boys and girls, can you imagine what it would have looked like to see an animal that could *breathe fire*?

Some people think that Leviathan was a kind of dinosaur that had a special hollow tube on his head, called a head crest. Others think that maybe the swimming monster Mosasaurus was the Leviathan. The fierce Mosasaurus was one of the biggest sea monsters ever! Whatever type of creature Leviathan was, it was not something with which you children would want to play. In fact, God asks a funny question to help us understand how scary this animal is. Do any of you boys or girls like to go fishing? Well, here is the question that God asks: "Would you want to go fishing and all of a sudden catch a Leviathan on your hook?" No, that would be really frightening!

Mosasaurus

Hooking a Leviathan

Do any of you girls and boys know what people called dinosaurs back in the old days, before the word dinosaur was invented? They were called *dragons*. Many different nations had stories about dragons. These stories from different parts of the world tell how scary and ferocious these great big, scaly animals were. And one of the things that some of these old stories would say is that dragons could *breathe fire*...just like the Leviathan in the Bible! The Babylonian people, the Indians, and the ancient Europeans all told about fiery dragons. Do you see the carving of a fire-breathing dragon that was made in the country of France in the 1500s?

Now if they were just making up silly stories, how come they all told stories about the same animal breathing fire, the dragon? Why didn't they make up a story about the fire-breathing dog? Or the fire-breathing duck? No, most likely they knew about real, fire-breathing dragons! But is it possible for an animal to *breathe fire* out its mouth without getting hurt? How can an animal have a fire inside him without being burned up?

French dragon carving

There is a special area of science that is called chemistry. This is the study of what natural things are made of and what happens when the different things come together. Special liquids or powders are called chemicals. Sometimes when we mix chemicals together, it doesn't do anything *very* interesting. Mixing milk and water just makes watery milk. But mixing vinegar and something called baking soda does something very interesting. As long as they are kept separate in the kitchen, they are fine. But if they are mixed, it causes a fizzy explosion to happen. Can you see the picture of Dino Dave doing this experiment? Maybe your parents would let you try this in your kitchen sometime.

Mixing baking soda and vinegar

Holding a Bombardier Beetle

Well, God made some plants and animals to have special chemicals that they can use to help protect themselves. A skunk makes a stinky chemical that he can spray on something that bothers him. Some plants, like poison ivy, make a chemical that gives us itchy bumps on our skin if we touch it. Dino Dave heard about an animal that uses chemicals to make an explosion, a much hotter one than even the vinegar and baking soda explosion that we can do in our kitchen. The animal is the Bombardier Beetle. The Bombardier Beetle has special chemicals in its body that it mixes together and then squirts out, causing an explosion. In the picture, you can see this happening.

Instead of having a tail on its back, the beetle has a special squirt gun that God made for it. That way it can aim the explosion in all different directions, under its stomach and even over its back!

So, if something is bothering this beetle, the nasty chemicals will squirt out at a fiery 212°, as hot as boiling water. This will burn whatever is bothering the beetle and chase it away. One day, a bombardier beetle landed on a boy's neck. When he tried to swat it away,

Beetle squirting underneath

the beetle burned his skin! Inside the Bombardier Beetle there are two separate containers that hold these special chemicals, so they don't mix until just the right time. This is like the vinegar and baking soda experiment we talked about. Isn't God's creation of this beetle something surprising and wonderful? This beetle could not have formed by chance. If one little thing was not right, the beetle would explode and kill itself!

Beetle squirting above

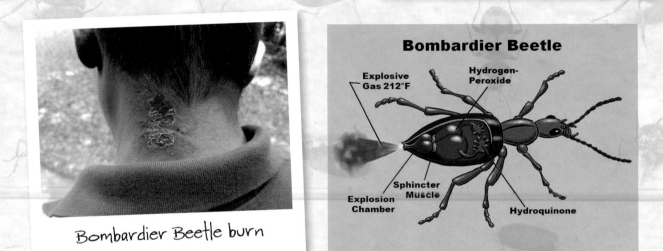
Bombardier Beetle burn

Bombardier Beetle

Explosive Gas 212°F

Hydrogen-Peroxide

Sphincter Muscle

Explosion Chamber

Hydroquinone

The Bombardier Beetle is a really amazing animal. It is kind of a *fiery* beetle, and it helps us to understand how a creature could *breathe fire* without getting hurt. Maybe the dragon's head had two containers of chemicals, just like the beetle has. Seeing an angry dragon would be scary enough. But can you imagine meeting a *fire-breathing* one? Why would God make such a fierce creature that could *breathe fire*? The Bible tells us that God made these creatures to teach us something about His power and greatness (Job 41:10). After God talked to Job about the Leviathan, Job understood how great God was, and he was sorry that he had questioned whether God knew about his troubles. He no longer doubted God's care for him. He said,

"I have heard of thee by the hearing of the ear: but now mine eye sees thee. Wherefore I...repent in dust and ashes" (Job 42:5-6).

You see, girls and boys, God is so much bigger and more powerful than any dinosaur. That means we need to be afraid to disobey Him. The Bible says,

"Fear God, and keep his commandments: for this is the whole duty of man" (Ecclesiastes 12:13).

But the Bombardier Beetle also tells us about God's care for a wonderful little animal to give it such a special protection. When we love the Lord and do what's right, like Job, we can trust God to take care of us. At the end of the book of Job, we see how God healed Job and helped him to get plenty of animals and more family. Job worshipped the Lord. He understood that God made big dinosaurs to show us about His power and how we should fear and respect Him!

DINO DAVE'S QUESTIONS

1. What sickness did Job have from the top of his head to the bottom of his feet? (Boils)

2. Do you remember the name of the fire-breathing monster in the book of Job? (Leviathan)

3. Which groups of people told stories of fire-breathing dragons? (The Babylonian people, the Indians and the ancient Europeans)

4. What is the area of science that studies the mixing of powders and liquids? (Chemistry)

5. What can we learn from the special protection God gave the Bombardier Beetle? (God will care for us if we love and fear Him.)

ADVENTURE 9

DINO DAVE & THE MURRAY MONSTER

(Lesson: God provides for us when we do His will and seek to praise Him.)

This is the story of Dino Dave and a fierce-looking animal that lives in a huge swamp in the country of Papua New Guinea (PNG). Some missionaries who were working with the people in PNG had built a church in the Lake Murray area. The pastor and another church leader saw a large, scary animal walking in the water near Boboa Island. They said it was as big as a truck and had skin like a crocodile. It walked on its two back legs and had tiny front legs. Its big mouth was full of sharp teeth. It seemed as if this monster was something like a T. rex! Dino Dave decided it was time to go on another expedition. What is an expedition? It is a trip to a faraway place to explore and learn things. Dino Dave was getting ready to travel to PNG to look for the Murray Monster.

Dino Dave packing for the trip

Dino Dave brought his friend Warren to be his helper for this long trip. They packed some of the same things that you might use if you were hiking and camping: a hammock, a sleeping bag, and dried food. Dino Dave also packed some unusual expedition tools. Do you see the taser in his hand? This is a special gun that can stop bad people and dangerous animals without killing them. Also, Dino Dave brought a night vision goggle. This special little machine helps people to see very clearly at night. Dino Dave printed off pictures of a few different dinosaurs. He hoped that these pictures would help him to find out exactly what type of monster was living in Lake Murray.

Early one morning Warren and Dino Dave boarded a jet and flew to the country of Australia. They stayed overnight in a town called Brisbane. There were fun animals to see: koalas, wallabies and kangaroos. For dinner, Dino Dave actually ate a kangaroo burger!

Warren with a kangaroo

The next morning, when he went to breakfast, he met a family from Australia who asked where they were going. "We are going to PNG to look for a living dinosaur," Dino Dave told them. The man laughed. "Don't you know that scientists have proved that all dinosaurs died 60 million years ago? They never lived with man!" Dino Dave shared with him how the Bible says God made the dinosaurs in the beginning along with the first people.

Lake Murray

Houses on stilts

Dugout canoe

The next day, the explorers flew on Air Niugini to Port Moresby, PNG. From there, they were supposed to take a flight to Lake Murray in the Western Province. Lake Murray is the largest lake in the country. It covers an area of about 700 square miles! The swamps and rivers are full of unexplored islands and deep pools. The people who live there have built villages on the small islands. Their houses stand off the ground on stilts so that the flood waters don't come into their homes. The people travel around in dugout canoes. They mainly eat fish. Missionaries had helped them to flatten the ground on one big island so that an airplane could land and take off. The planes brought in school supplies, clothes, and medicine. Dino Dave was supposed to fly into that little airport.

However, Dino Dave and Warren learned that their flight was canceled. They waited in a line with other people for four hours, hoping to catch a different airplane. But the man at the airline desk said they would have to come back and try again the next day. They were very sad! Would they ever make it to Lake Murray? Dino Dave decided to pray and claim the promise of God to direct their way. The Bible says,

Airport official & Warren

"Trust in the LORD with all thine heart; and lean not unto thine own understanding. In all thy ways acknowledge him, and he shall direct thy paths" (Proverbs 3:5-6).

What does it mean to acknowledge God? It means to ask for His guidance and believe that He can help. Finally, after waiting for two days, a missionary plane landed, and the pilot agreed to take the two explorers to Lake Murray. Dino Dave immediately thanked God. When God answers our prayer, it is important that we remember to praise Him.

Dino Dave took his backpack up to the little plane and sat in the co-pilot's seat. Off they went! After flying for a long time, they saw the swamps of Lake Murray from the airplane window. Then the plane bumped down onto the grass and came to a stop. Dino Dave happily got out and lifted up his backpack. Finally, he and Warren were at Lake Murray! Although the people were friendly, it took a while to find someone who could speak English to be their guide. They hired a man named Andrew, along with some of his helpers. After that, they rented a boat to take them around the lake to Boboa Island, where the monster had been seen. They found a grassy place to camp. It rained on Dino Dave as he hung his hammock from the trees. Warren lit a fire to cook some food.

Many islanders came by to talk. A few of the people had seen the Murray Monster. They looked carefully at all of Dino Dave's pictures and pointed to the Ceratosaurus. That dinosaur had spikes going down its back and a very strong tail. One hunter told the story of seeing the creature up close. He came acrosss it while hunting far up one of the rivers.

Copilot Dino Dave

Dino Dave, Warren & guides

Campsite on Boboa Island

Eye witness

Hunting dogs and dinosaur

Lake Murray villagers

His dogs began barking loudly and scared it away. Dino Dave asked him if the monster had left behind any footprints. The hunter nodded and drew a large track with three toes in the ground. The next day, Dino Dave and Warren were excited to explore. They boarded the boat and told their guide Andrew to take them to other islands where they could talk to more people. Instead, to their surprise, the guide drove the boat back to the main island with the airport. Dino Dave wondered if the guide did not understand.

As they neared the shore Dino Dave could see a large group of people gathered, Including the big village chief. They were talking excitedly in their language and pointing at Dino Dave and Warren. Dino Dave began to pray quietly to himself. "God, help us! If they want to hurt us, please let us escape. Don't let them take all the things we need to finish our trip." Dino Dave told Warren to stay on the boat with the backpacks and pray while he went with Andrew to the chief. The leader demanded to be paid a lot of money to let the Americans camp on the land! Dino Dave explained kindly that he had only brought money to buy food, rent the boat and to pay guides. It had already cost extra money to get plane tickets. He told the villagers that this expedition was not from a big university, but just two men who loved Jesus and wanted to find out about the dinosaur. When the people heard that Dino Dave loved Jesus, they became calm. They had learned about Jesus from the missionary. The people were not happy to get no money, but they let Dino Dave get back in the boat and go.

Warren happily thanked God for helping them. Dino Dave remembered a favorite Bible verse.

"Call upon me in the day of trouble: I will deliver thee, and thou shalt glorify me" (Psalm 50:15).

What does it mean to glorify God? It means to tell Him how wonderful He is. It means to talk to others about His great works. It means to sing of Him in our time of worship. Each morning, Dino Dave, Warren and their guides sat around the campfire after breakfast. They read a little bit from the Bible and prayed. Dino Dave even explained to the guides how to become a Christian by believing in Jesus.

Missionary plane

During the day, Dino Dave and Warren traveled around the lake and talked to people. They met other villagers who had seen the dinosaur in the lake. They learned that the monster swims quickly by moving his tail like a crocodile. It catches and eats fish. At night, the explorers stayed up late and looked out over Lake Murray with their night vision. The time in PNG passed so quickly. Soon the day came for Warren and Dino Dave to go back to the grassy airport and take a plane to Australia. They had not seen the Murray Monster or its footprints. However, God protected them on their travels, allowed them to share the love of Jesus, and brought them safely back home. Dino Dave thanked God for being with them on the expedition and directing their paths.

Dino Dave's Questions

1. What country does the Murray Monster live in? (Papua New Guinea)

2. What is the name for the special gun that Dino Dave has to stop bad people and dangerous animals without killing them? (Taser)

3. What does it mean to acknowledge God in our life?
   (It means to ask for His guidance and believe He can help.)

4. Did Dino Dave pay the chief just to camp on the land? (No)

5. When God answers our prayer, what do we need to do?
   (Thank and praise Him)

63

ADVENTURE 10

DINO DAVE & SALTY SEAS

(Lesson: Studying the waters that flow into the salty oceans tell us that the Earth is young.)

Too salty

What is the small container pictured up above? That's right, it is an upside-down saltshaker. Salt is falling out and going somewhere down below. Down there something is getting more and more salty because of the salt that is pouring onto it. Maybe it is falling onto some food that's getting really salty! We can tell if there is a lot of salt in something just by tasting it. Even a baby can tell if something is too salty...and they don't like it. Sometimes, even if a thing tastes good, it can be changed to taste bad by adding too much salt.

I would like to suggest doing a little experiment today to help us see if we can taste just a little bit of salt in water. Let's take four drinking cups. We will pour the same amount of warm water into all of them. Then I'm going to ask a couple of volunteers to step out for just a minute. I'm going to put just a little teaspoonful of salt in two of them. Then you each will each have a chance to taste both salty and regular to see if you can tell us which one is normal water and which one is saltwater. Ready? Let's try it! Boys and girls, our mouths are very good at tasting salt. Some people's tongues are so good at tasting that they can tell if there is just a pinch of salt in a whole gallon of water!

Have you ever been to the ocean to swim? Did you ever get your head dunked under the water? What does the water in the ocean taste like? That's right. Sea water tastes really salty...just like the salt in those water cups we just tested. Did you know that some parts of the ocean are saltier than others? Dino Dave has traveled to many different places and tasted ocean water from Australia to America, from the Atlantic, the Pacific, the Mediterranean,

Getting a mouthful of seawater

the Caribbean, and the Indian Seas! And guess what? He found that all these oceans taste yucky salty!

Why is seawater salty? How did the oceans get that way? Below is a picture that helps us to understand what happens that makes the oceans so salty. Rain falls on the mountains and as it goes down through the rocks in the ground, it melts some of the salt in the rocks. This little bit of salt stays in the water as it goes into the brooks, and then into the big rivers, and finally into the ocean. Then the warm sunshine makes pure water come up into the air from the ocean (something we call evaporation) and leaves the salt behind in the sea. That evaporated water is carried as clouds back to the mountain where it rains down again. This rising of the water up out of the oceans, raining in the mountains, and going back down to the oceans is talked about in the Bible. Ecclesiastes 1:7 says,

Dino Dave tasting seawater

"All the rivers run into the sea; yet the sea is not full; unto the place from whence the rivers come, thither they return again."

The water going up and down constantly carries more salt into the world's oceans.

So, every year the oceans get more and more and *more* salty. It is almost as if someone with a huge saltshaker were pouring salt into the ocean. Today the sea is almost 4% salt. But girls and boys, we can learn an important lesson from studying salty seas. People who do not believe what God's Word says in the book of Genesis like to think that the Earth is very, very old. Billions of years old.

Ocean Salinity is about 3.6%.

Atmospheric & Volcanic Dust

Rivers, Glaciers

Erosion

Halite Deposition

Spray

Seepage

Ion Exchange

Ocean

Sediments

Vents

Continents

Seafloor Basalts

But the salty seas help us to see that the Earth is *not* billions of years old. If every year the ocean gets a little bit saltier than the year before, we can measure how much new salt comes into the oceans every year. Then we can know how many years ago the oceans started out with fresh water (no salt at all). If the Earth were really 4 billion years old, the sea would be a *lot* saltier than it is today.

Salt formations, Dead Sea

Do you know what is the saltiest sea on earth? It is a place called the Dead Sea. This big lake between the countries of Israel and Jordan is about

Dino Dave in the Dead Sea

34% salt! The Bible calls this the "Salt Sea" (Genesis 14:3). There is so much salt that no fish can live there. That's why it's called the Dead Sea. Salt settles to the bottom in layers of goo and forms weird shapes by the shore. When Dino Dave went swimming in the Dead Sea, he got just a little bit of water in his eyes and it burned like fire! The water is so thick with salt that people float on the top of the lake without even swimming. You can sit in the water and just paddle around. Water comes into the Dead Sea from the Jordan River, but there is no river going out.

There is a *lot* of salt in the rocks in the ground. Sometimes there are whole rock layers that are white with salt. For thousands of years, people have been digging into the ground to find salt and bring it up in big chunks. Then salt is broken up into very tiny pieces so that we can put it into our saltshakers and use it on our food. The places where people dig up salt are called salt mines. Did you know that there are huge salt mines under the big American city of Detroit, Michigan? This mine was producing 8,000 tons of rock salt each month in 1914. There are 100 miles of mining roads underneath the city of Detroit still today.

Dead Sea salt layers

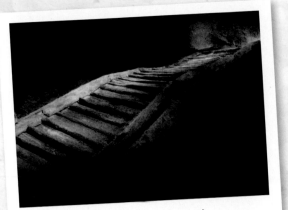

Stairs to ancient salt mine

Digging in an ancient salt mine

Salt was mined back when Jesus was alive. Here is a picture of stairs going down into a very old salt mine in Austria. The workers would carefully chop out large chunks of salt to be carried to the surface. In fact, salt was so valuable in the days when the Bible was written, that sometimes the Roman government would pay people with salt instead of money. The Bible says,

"Let your speech be always with grace, seasoned with salt, that ye may know how ye ought to answer every man" (Colossians 4:6).

When we talk, our words should be careful and valuable, just like the salt.

Salt is an important thing to have in our bodies. It's OK to put a little salt on an egg or some meat. Job 6:6 in the Bible says that things that do not have much taste need to have some salt, things like an egg. So sometimes salt makes things so much yummier for us to eat! Jesus said that Christians are to be the "salt of the earth" (Matthew 5:13). How can a person be like salt? Are we supposed to be human saltshakers bouncing up and down and spinning around, salting everywhere? No. But there are certain things about salt that help us to understand what we should do for Jesus. Salt gives flavor to foods that have little to no taste. Christians should be different from the people around them who don't love God. They should stand out in a good way and be noticed...just as the salty water in our experiment was different. God likes it when we help our friends do what's right.

Also, salt preserves things. If you don't put meat into the refrigerator, it will soon start to rot and decay. Then you can't eat it. We say it is "spoiled." Making it cold (in the refrigerator) helps to preserve it so that it will not spoil. But long before people had refrigerators, they learned that putting

Salt preserves fish

salt on food keeps it from spoiling. See the picture of salted fish? After being salted, the fish will last for over a year, instead of just for a few days. Christians are supposed to help to keep things around us from spoiling. We should stop the rot and decay and badness in our world. Are you children acting like the salt of the earth? Are you making a good difference in the world around you? What are some "everyday" things that boys and girls can do to be like salt? Probably you could tell other people about Jesus; be an example of obeying authority; clean up messes and pick up garbage; encourage friends to be kind to each other; or help someone who needs something.

DINO DAVE'S QUESTIONS

1. Is it true that just a pinch of salt can be tasted in a whole gallon of water? (Yes)

2. With all the new salt coming into the ocean every year, could the Earth really be billions of years old? (No)

3. What is the saltiest sea in the world? (The Dead Sea)

4. What book in the Bible says it is OK to put a little salt on our eggs? (Job)

5. What are some of the things that you can do to be salt? (Tell other people about Jesus, be an example of obeying, clean up messes, encourage friends to be kind, or help someone.)

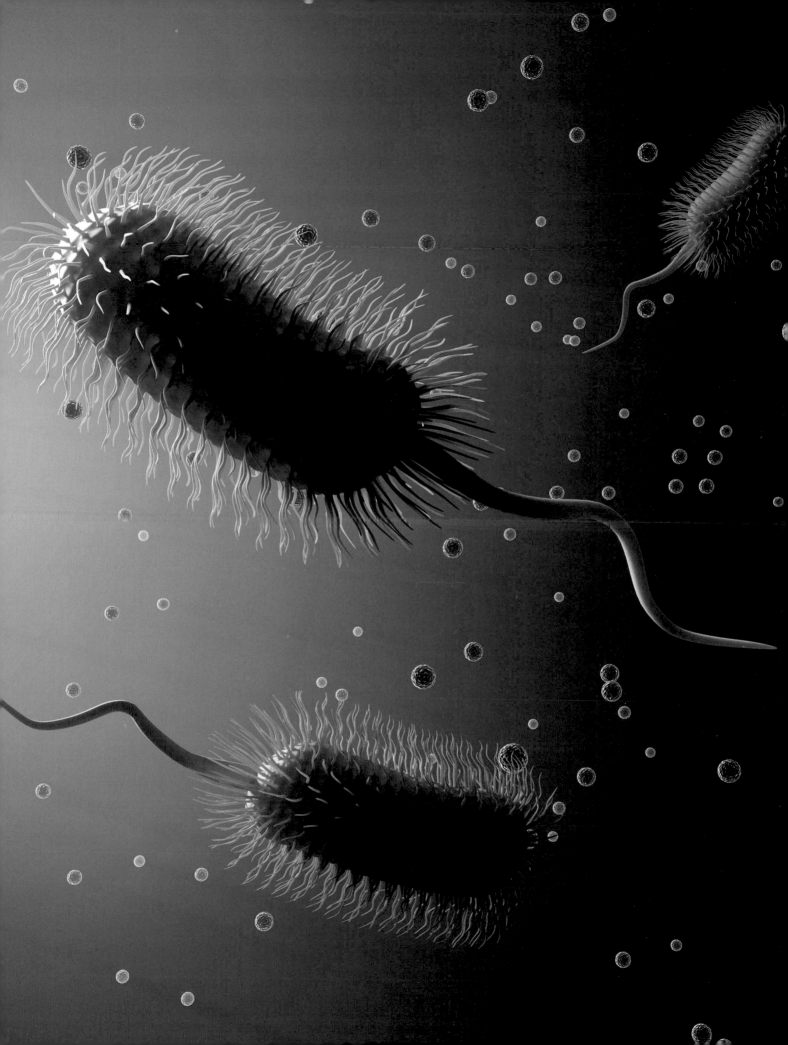

DINO DAVE & THE FANTASTIC FLAGELLUM

(Lesson: A tiny machine in bacteria teaches us about God's care for us.)

Viewing bacteria in the microscope

What are these little swimmy fellows with the long tail in the picture? That is a tiny kind of creature called bacteria. All living things are made of cells, but bacteria have only one cell in their whole body. It is soooooo tiny that 150,000 of them could rest on the tip of one of your hairs! We can see these small creatures in a special machine called a microscope. The microscope lets us see things, tiny things that are "microscopic," that we could never see with just our human eyes,

The Bible tells us that we should stop and look at all the creatures that God made to see what we can learn from them. Job 12:7-8 says,

"But ask now the beasts, and they shall teach thee; and the fowls of the air, and they shall tell thee: Or speak to the earth, and it shall teach thee: and the fishes of the sea shall declare unto thee."

Each of these animals teach us about God and His work of creation. But today I don't want to just talk about tiny bacteria creatures. I want to especially talk about that long tail that is on the back of the bacteria. This tail has an important job to do. It moves the bacteria forward through water, almost like swimming. This tail has a special name. It is called a flagellum. Today I want to tell you all about that fantastic flagellum.

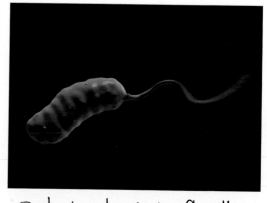
Bacterium & spinning flagellum

Have any of you children ever gone swimming in a swimming pool? When we swim, we push ourselves through the water with our hands and our feet. Some people can swim fast by kicking and moving their hands just right. But we can go through the water a lot faster if we get into a speedboat. The speedboat has a special kind of motor that goes down into the water. It is built to be able to move a boat through water very quickly. How does the motor do this? Dino Dave decided to find someone who works with boat motors so he could learn more.

Swimming in the ocean

In the picture, Dino Dave is with a man named Phil, who likes working on boat motors. Dino Dave asked him what it is like to work on motors that push boats through the water. Phil said that boat motors are special. They are different from car or motorcycle motors because they must be able to get wet. Some of the parts are up in the air just above the water and some of the parts are down under the water. Outboard boat motors are also very complicated. They have *lots* of different pieces. If one little piece is missing or broken, the boat might only move very slowly, or maybe the motor will not even work at all. Dino Dave had a good time visiting with Phil and learning about motorboats. Dino Dave likes driving motorboats. Wow, they can go fast! Have any of you children taken a ride in a speedboat?

Phil & Dino Dave

Look at the picture of a boat's outboard motor. You can see the engine up above the water. The engine burns gasoline and turns a long metal rod called the driveshaft. The driveshaft goes from the engine up top all the way down to the bottom part that rests under the water. There the driveshaft turns something called a propeller. The propeller spins in the water and pushes the water back, just as your hands do when you are swimming through the water. This propeller makes the boat go forward.

Dino Dave & DNA in a motorboat

72

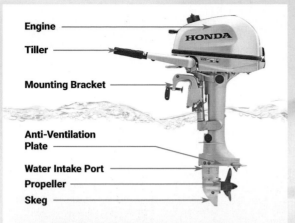

Engine

Tiller

Mounting Bracket

Anti-Ventilation Plate

Water Intake Port

Propeller

Skeg

Do you see the picture of an outboard motor that is all taken apart? There are 500 different parts! Phil is right...a boat motor can be very complicated. All of those exact pieces have to be put in just the right place all at the same time, or the motor will not run properly.

But thousands of years before man invented the first outboard boat motor, God had already built a complicated outboard motor. That's right! The motor that God built is the tiny tail that helps bacteria to swim through the water. We talked about that at the beginning of the story. Does anyone remember the name for that tail? It is called a flagellum! In Genesis 1:21 the Bible says,

"And God created great whales, and every living creature that moveth, which the waters brought forth abundantly."

God made all the things that swim in the water, big creatures like whales and tiny creatures like bacteria. Then next thing Dino Dave wanted to learn was how does the bacteria flagellum work? How does it swim through water?

Dino Dave decided to talk with a type of scientist called a microbiologist. A microbiologist studies living things that are very small that can only be seen through a microscope. Dino Dave had a conversation with a microbiologist called Dr. Kevin Anderson. Dr. Anderson has worked for the US Government and has studied different bacteria. He told Dino Dave that the flagellum is a very complicated outboard motor. The tail spins around kind of like a boat propeller so that it can push the bacteria through the water. It can spin very quickly. We measure how fast something spins by counting how many times it can turn completely around in one minute. This is really important to know if you want to go quickly. If a propeller that is pushing water can turn around faster, than it makes the boat go faster. So, people that make boat motors talk about how many times the propeller turns or revolves around each minute. This is called "revolutions per minute" or rpm. A fast outboard motor on a boat can go up to 10,000 rpm. But the fantastic flagellum that God made has a motor that does 100,000 rpm!

Dr. Anderson & Dino Dave

There are many different kinds of bacteria that have a flagellum. Some bacteria even have more than one flagellum. This allows the bacteria to travel even faster. We have speedboats that also use multiple motors to go quicker. But the fantastic flagellum can do something special. It can stop spinning in a quarter of a turn and change directions to go backwards. No outboard motor that we make can do that! Dr. Anderson told Dino Dave that he would put bacteria in a drip of water onto a flat glass slide under a microscope. Then he would put one spec of sugar on the slide. He would watch the bacteria all swim over to the sugar. The bacteria can sense where the food is just as you can smell when your mom is cooking your favorite dinner in the kitchen. Bacteria have an amazing outboard motor that runs better than the motors that people can make. Oh yes, it really is a fantastic flagellum!

Boat with multiple motors

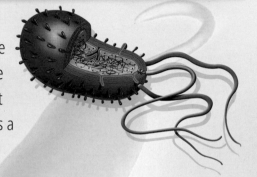

Do you remember the picture showing all the parts that are in an outboard motor? Well, the bacteria flagellum has lots of parts too. There are more than 40 different parts that have to be in the exact right place at the exact same time. Otherwise, the flagellum motor will not work, and the bacteria will be stuck going nowhere. When we look at all of these parts, we recognize them because they do the same thing as the parts in the outboard motors that people build. Dr. Anderson was right. The bacteria motor is very complicated. People who do not believe that God created the world say that a bacteria flagellum came together by chance. But the 40 parts are very special things (called proteins) that are built in a special order, just for the flagellum. This is a lot like the way that we build special parts for a boat motor. This could not happen all by itself. Someone had to think of it and put it together. The bacteria flagellum is an example of an amazing machine that works in a single cell. There are many other wonderful microscopic machines like this in living things. As we learn about them, we see the wisdom of our Creator God.

But there is another lesson we can learn by looking at the flagellum. If God cares so much about tiny bacteria that He gives them a fantastic flagellum to cause them to swim through water, don't you think He can take care of your needs?

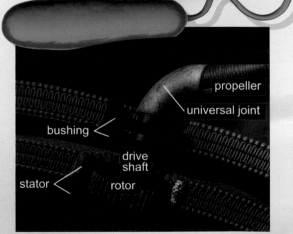

propeller
universal joint
bushing
drive shaft
stator
rotor

74

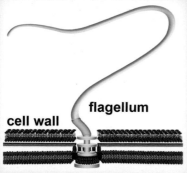

cell wall · flagellum

When Jesus was talking to his disciples, He taught them not to worry. He said,

"But even the very hairs of your head are all numbered" (Luke 12:7).

Jesus was showing that God cared for little things like hairs and knew exactly the number of them. But God also takes care of even tinier things, like bacteria that we can only see with a microscope. He is a good God that loves each of you boys and girls, and He has great wisdom to be able to take care of His children!

DINO DAVE'S QUESTIONS

1. What does it mean to be microscopic?
   (Something is so tiny that it takes a microscope to see it.)

2. Is a boat's outboard engine very complicated?
   (Yes, there are lots of different parts.)

3. Which can turn around more times in a minute, the flagellum or a boat motor? (The flagellum)

4. Could the 40 special protein parts of the flagellum come together by themselves? (No, they were designed by God.)

5. Jesus taught that God cares for even the tiny things about us. What part of our body does God number and count?
   (The hairs of our head)

ADVENTURE 12

DINO DAVE & THE TEXAS TRACKS

(Lesson: Human tracks in rock beside dinosaur tracks tell us about the creation & catastrophe.)

Not long ago, Dino Dave visited the ocean and was walking on the beach. When people walk in wet sand or in mud, their feet usually squish into the ground, and they leave behind a mark in the ground. We call this a track or footprint. Have you ever left footprints that look like that? Maybe you went out and stepped in the mud after it rained. Or maybe you saw a cat or dog make some tracks in the soft dirt. In the picture to the left is a footprint of an animal with three toes, something *really big*. Can you guess what animal made this footprint? That's a dinosaur footprint! It left tracks in the wet mud many years ago.

Dino Dave's tracks in the sand

Tracks like these usually do not stay there very long. If it is at the beach, a wave may come and wash them away. If it is in your backyard, dirt may get blown onto it. Or the sides of the track will begin to dry out and crumble down. Or someone else might step on top of it and then it will disappear. The only way to get tracks to stay for a long time is if the wet muddy layer is like cement and hardens very quickly. That usually doesn't happen just in sand or backyard mud. It does happen when a special mud or volcanic ash is spread onto the land and something steps into it.

A dog walking in wet cement

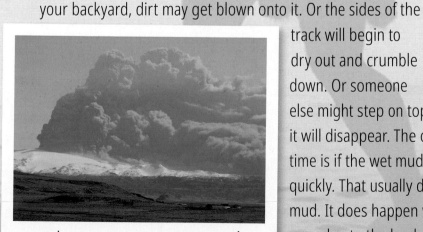

Volcanic ash spreading out

77

Then the mud with the footprints hardens into rock. But even these stone tracks won't last for a really long time, unless they are buried by another layer to protect and preserve them. Otherwise, the rain, wind and snow will wear the rock layer away. We call this erosion. There is a special word for the huge floods and volcanoes that spread big ash or mud layers onto the land. These events are called "catastrophes."

Did you know that scientists have found *lots* of tracks of dinosaurs and other animals in the rock layers? All of these fossil footprints in the rock layers around the Earth tell us that there was a *big* catastrophe in the past that washed huge amounts of mud onto the land. Then different animals made tracks in it, and then more mud was washed on top of those tracks and preserved them. Can anyone remember what was this huge catastrophe in Earth's past? It was the great Flood that the Bible talks about in the book of Genesis. The Bible says that first the low, flat land was covered with water, then all the hills were covered with water and then "the mountains were covered" (Genesis 7:17-20). Each time the waves would come in, the water would go higher. So, people and animals that were trying to get away from the water to a safe place would climb higher up and they would leave footprints in the mud layers.

Dinosaur fossil footprints

Often, the dinosaur tracks that we find fossilized in the rocks are all going in one direction. It is as if all the dinosaurs were running away from something...maybe big waves! Another thing that is interesting is that some dinosaur tracks start sunken very deep in the rock. But then, as they are running forward, the tracks get higher and higher in the ground until there is just a small scrape in the rock. What does this tell us about the dinosaur who made these tracks? This is what would happen if a dinosaur was trying to run away from the flood water, but it was getting lifted up by a big wave. First, it was running and leaving deep tracks. Then as the water carried it up, it started swimming and leaving only faint scratches in the ground.

Dinosaur tracks in the same direction

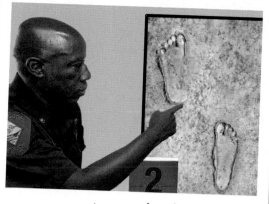
Track investigation

We can learn a lot just from studying footprints. Footprints tell us what walked through an area and maybe even when it was there. Each person's footprint is different. So, when the police are looking for someone who did something bad, they will sometimes use footprints to help them find the bad person. That's how footprints can be important clues for knowing what happened.

Dino Dave heard about some fossil footprints that were found in the state of Texas. This is an area where there are oh so many dinosaur tracks. In fact, because there are so many tracks in the area of Glen Rose, Texas, the government made it into a special park: Dinosaur Valley State Park. Dino Dave decided to visit this area and see what he could learn from these Texas Tracks. First, Dino Dave traveled to Texas on a big airplane. Then he got in a car and drove down to the city of Glen Rose. This area is like a desert with lots of sand and beautiful rocks. These rocks are fun for children to climb on, but they can also be the home of a rattle snake!

Big Rock Park

Finally, Dino Dave arrived at the Dinosaur Valley State Park. He was very excited to see some big dinosaurs that someone had put by the parking lot. Then he read the sign in front of the dinosaurs. It said that the park's tracks were made by *Acrocanthosaurus*, a dinosaur that lived 140 million years ago. People who do not believe what the Bible says in Genesis think that the dinosaurs lived and walked around many millions of years before there were

any people. But Dino Dave believes the Bible. The book of Genesis says that God made the "creeping thing, and beast of the earth" the same day He made Adam, the first man (Genesis 1:24-26).

Dino Dave saw some of the beautiful dinosaur tracks in the park. Look at the picture on the next page of the big dinosaur footprints in stone. Some are so big that they could be a bathtub (top of p. 77)!

Acrocanthosaurus tracks

The Paluxy River in the summer

What do you think we can learn from tracks like these? Well, we can learn how big the dinosaur was, what direction it was walking, and if it walked slowly or was running. Some of these famous tracks were even cut out of the rock and taken to a museum in New York City. Dino Dave heard about some extra special tracks found down by the Paluxy River. The river was very dry in the summer when Dino Dave hiked down there. On the sides of this river are many dinosaur footprints. Right next to them, in the State Park, a fossil footprint was found that looks just like a human footprint. What can we learn from this fossil?

We can learn that many years ago, while the mud was still soft, both people and dinosaurs walked through this area. Then the mud hardened into rock, just like cement. After that you couldn't leave tracks there anymore because it was hard stone.

Look again at the picture on p. 76. The dinosaur stepped into the same place in the mud where the person had just stepped! What can we learn from these Texas Tracks? Both people and dinosaurs were running away from the waves of the great Flood. The people who do not believe the Bible like to say that *all* the dinosaurs were already dead by the time there were people to walk around. But the Texas Tracks show us that people and dinosaurs were walking there at the same time.

The same week that Dino Dave visited the Texas Tracks, some scientists were digging down through rocks and sand to try and find more human tracks. Dino Dave was able to stay and help them.

Not far away from these Texas Tracks, another special footprint was discovered. Scientists were studying animal tracks in some very old limestone. But a fossil human footprint called the Zapata track was discovered in that same rock layer! That means that people were around from the beginning, just as Jesus said in Mark 10:6. Jesus knows exactly what happened in the beginning! John 1:3 says,

"All things were made by him; and without him was not any thing made that was made."

The next time you see footprints, think about what they can teach you. Tracks are like clues about the past. The Texas Tracks help people learn about creation and the Genesis Flood!

Dino Dave on the dig line

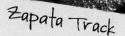

Zapata Track

DINO DAVE'S QUESTIONS

1. Do the tracks that we make in the mud or sand last a long time? (No)

2. What catastrophe spread out huge mud layers like cement for animals to make tracks in? (The Flood)

3. Which state has so many tracks that they made a special park? (Texas)

4. Are human footprints found in the same fossilized mud layers as dinosaur tracks? (Yes)

5. Who said that God made people right in the beginning? (Jesus)

PICTURE CREDITS

Chapter 1 Dino Dave & the Cryptid Champ

1. Plesiosaur profile image by StockTrek Images
2. Background Plesiosaurus skeleton by CG Studio
3. Background Tanystropheus skeleton by Wikimedia
4. Background Pliosaurus skeleton by Prehistoric Wiki
5. Background Futabasaurus skeleton by BrantWorks
6. Champ photo by Sandra Mansi
7. Girl hiding under blanket by Shutterstock
8. Monitor picture by Spiegel
9. Giant Squid by Infobae
10. Plesiosaurus picture by Shutterstock
11. Kraken attacking ship by Samuel Allan
12. Colossal Squid photo by Blue Planet Archive
13. Egyptians capturing plesiosaur by Dobbs
14. Egyptian comparison to plesiosaur after Microsoft
15. Dino Dave at Lake Champlain by Jeff Andrew
16. Video of Champ by ABC News
17. Notebook graphic by DepositPhotos

Chapter 2 Dino Dave & La Grand'Goule

1. St. George Slaying the Dragon by Gardner Museum
2. Misty scene after Shutterestock
3. Dimorphodon flying after Jurassic World
4. La Grand'Goule by Sainte-Croix Museum
5. Sainte-Croix Abbey by Service des Moniales
6. La GrandGoule procession by Limedia Galeries
7. Frankish Warrior after Sarka Photos
8. Dimorphodon pterosaur after DK Images
9. Disintegrating Walls of Jerusalem by Generation Word
10. Warren's Shaft (Dragon Well) by WikiMedia
11. Bator Dragon photos by Dave Woetzel
12. Wawel Cathedral dragon bones by 123RF
13. Aldrovandus by Alamy
14. Ulysses & Dragon by Taylor

Chapter 3 Dino Dave & Rationalist Rick

1. Rationalist Rick poses by Ricky Rush
2. Background wet concrete by Shutterstock
3. Garage construction and animatronic dinosaur photos by Dave Woetzel
4. Jesus image by GoodSoil
5. The Parable of Two Builder pictures after Twinkl
6. Sunrise & the Bible by iStock

Chapter 4 Dino Dave & the Complicated Cell

1. Portrait Louis Pasteur by WikiMedia
2. Background amoebas and Cactus plant by 123RF
3. Human cell, cell division, yorkie, and moldy soup by Shutterstock
4. Baby Jeremiah photo credit Primark
5. Stuffed dinosaur by JÄTTELIK
6. Soup and Stone by DepositPhotos
7. Ant by Jon Lieff
8. E Coli by David Mack – Getty Images
9. Dino Dave picture, canned soup, pasteurized dairy, and holding watch parts by Dave Woetzel

10. Louis Pasteur painting by Robert Thom
11. Cell & Organelles after YourGenome.org
12. Medieval walled city after WikiMedia
13. Pocket Watch by MasterHorologer

Chapter 5 Dino Dave & Fossil Fuels

1. Sinclair fuel station WI Dells by Alamy
2. Background oil gusher by History.com
3. Sinclair logo and oil truck by Sinclair Corporation
4. Sinclair filling station, Dino Dave riding a green dinosaur, and John Morris by Dave Woetzel
5. Tar seep, algae, and coal with fern by WikiMedia
6. Moses in ark by Normons
7. Drilling Rig and Oil Refinery by DreamsTime
8. Grasshopper pump and Oil gusher by Shutterstock
9. Algae to fuel by PNNL
10. Chinese drilling for natural gas and bamboo piping from Zhong & Huang
11. Oil well in Egypt by Praxis

Chapter 6 Dino Dave & the Lava Layers

1. Volcanic mountain by DepositPhotos
2. Hot magma background by Dreamstime
3. Volcano Diagram after Alamy
4. Testing lava by Dickinson College
5. Lava flowing into the sea and Rainbow over Bryce Canyon by Shutterstock
6. Hawaii pictures and Mount St. Helens ash by Dave Woetzel
7. Mauna Loa road by Geotripper Images
8. Kilauea flow by USA Today

9. Mauna Loa lava layer erosion by Geotripper Images
10. Plants growing in lava by Fast Pic
11. Lava lizard by Kim Clune
12. Hawaii lava layer growing flowers by NPS
13. Pocket Gopher by USFS, Charlie Crisafulli
14. Mount St. Helens Explodes by USGS
15. Pumice Plain in 1980 by WikiMedia
16. Pumice Plain in 2015 by Alamy
17. Mud flow in Brazil by Fox News
18. Conforming Rock layers by Hive Miner
19. Rainbow layer cake by Taste of Home

Chapter 7 Dino Dave & the Midnight Moon

1. Rocket launch with Moon and Background Earthrise by Shutterstock
2. Moon photo and Galileo image by Wikimedia
3. Moon rising and Telescope looking at the Moon by Alamy
4. Garth photo and Cape Canaveral pictures by Dave Woetzel
5. Craters on the Moon by Laurent Langelez
6. Moon crater comparison by The Tribune India
7. Saturn Rocket, astronauts, and Lunar Module by NASA
8. Swinging a ball by Wired
9. Apollo Pacific landing by Mind Games
10. Moon's orbit after Foter

Chapter 8 Dino Dave & the Bombardier Beetle

1. Bombardier Beetle vertical graphic by Science Friday
2. Background beetles by Pixabay
3. Small, faded beetle image by Alamy

3. Dinosaur track bathtub by Aaron Judkins

4. Dino Dave pictures and Paluxy are photos by Dave Woetzel

5. Dog walks in wet cement by Pikabu

6. Eyjafjallajokull Volcano ash plume by WikiMedia

7. Ark and drowning dinosaurs by Lavoie

8. CO Dinosaur tracks by Dreamstime

9. Chinese Dinosaur tracks by China.org.cn

10. Police officer pointing photo after Keith Hayes

11. Big Rock Park photo after Visit Granbury

12. Brachiosaurus and man running after Dreamstime

13. Zapata track by Don Patton